I Can

Carousel Readers

Beryl Smith

Illustrated by Mary Ann Zapalac

Dominie Press, Inc.

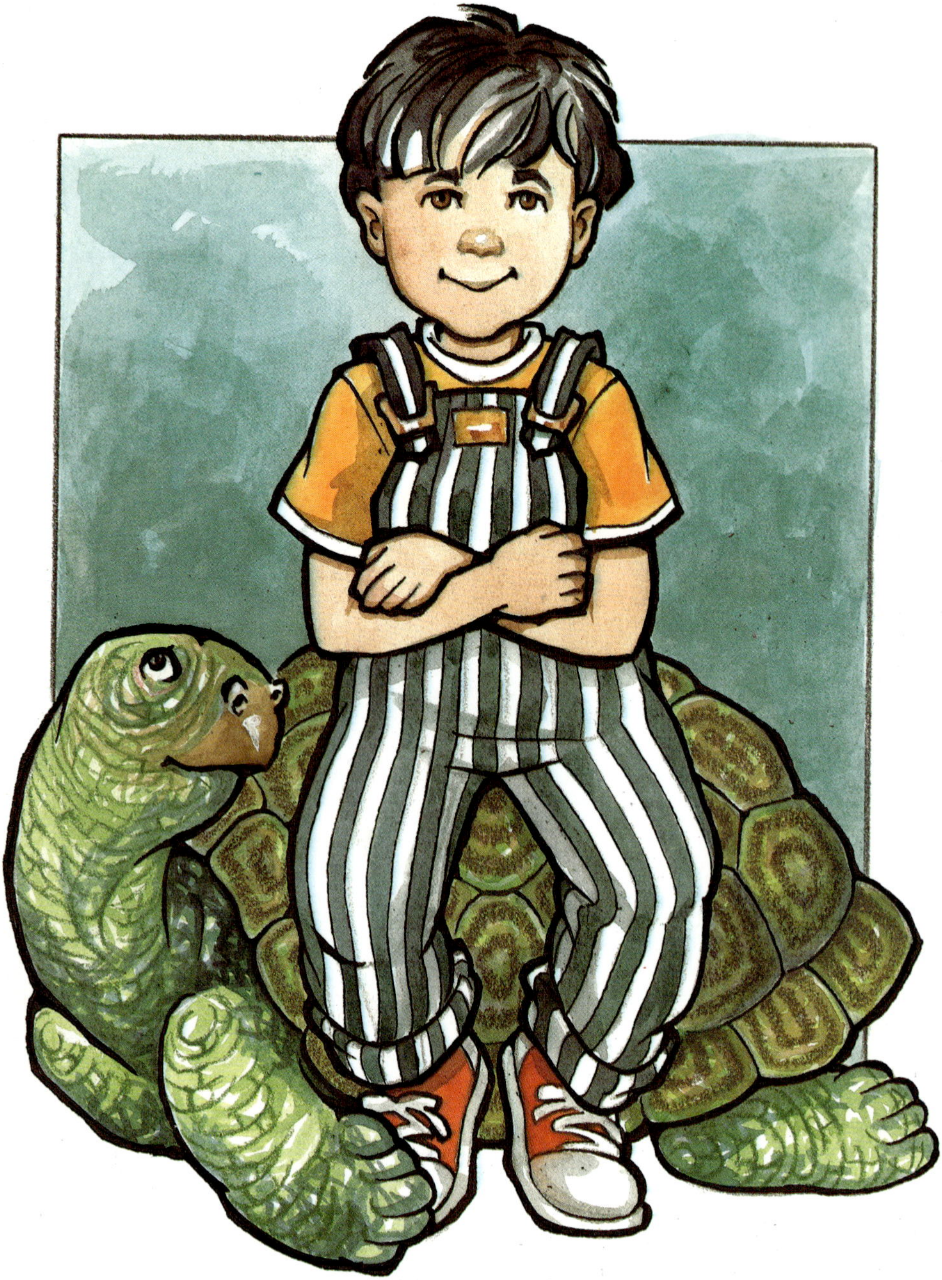

I can sit.

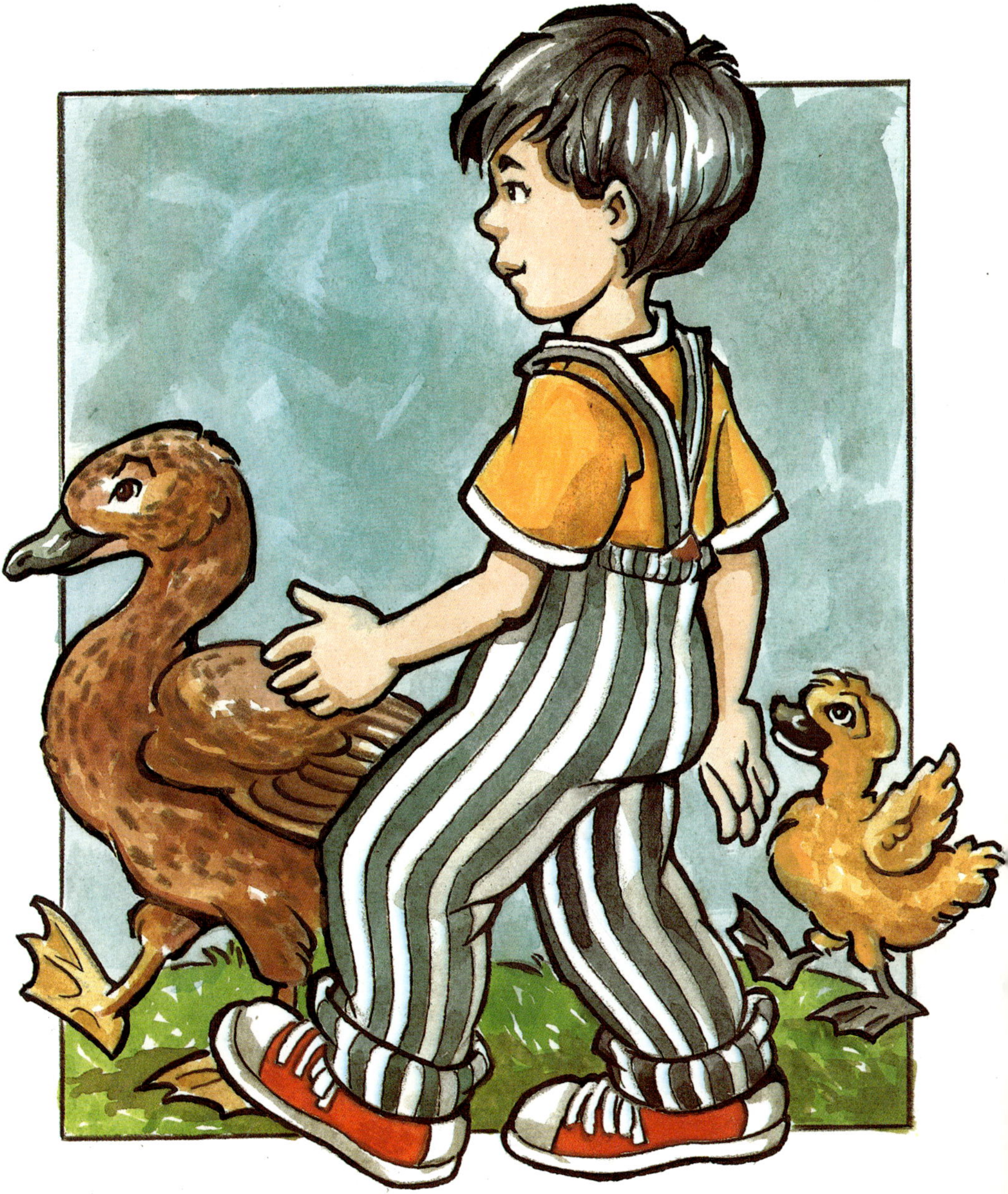

I can walk.

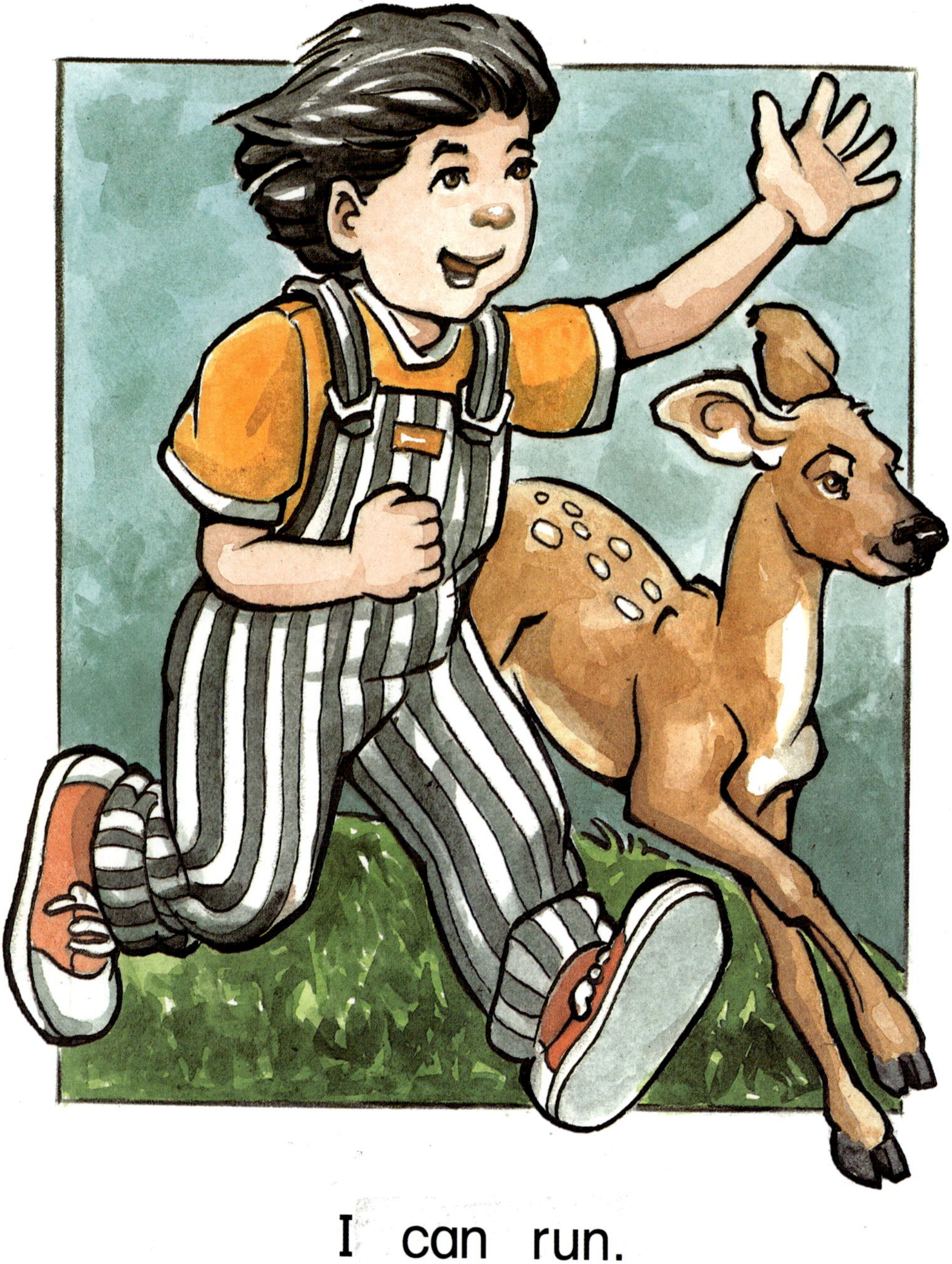

I can run.

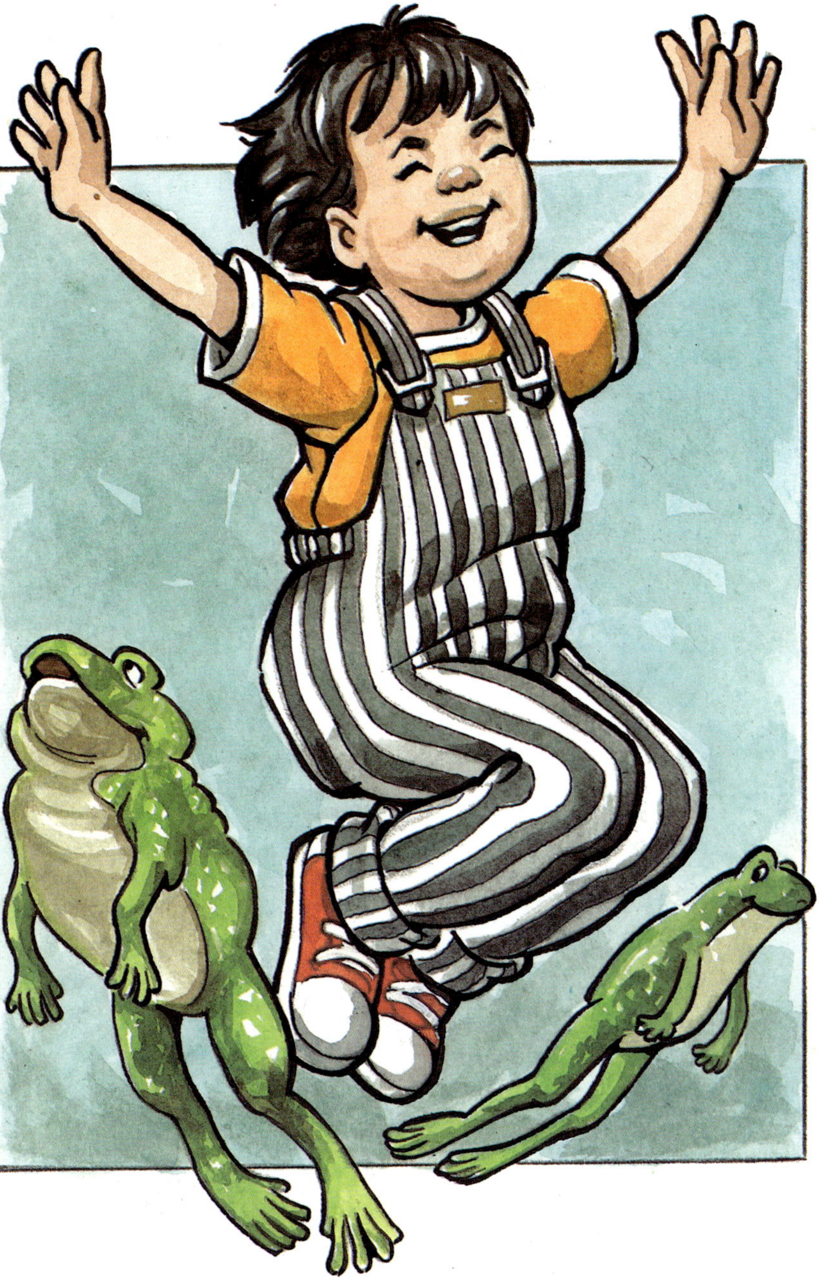

I can jump.

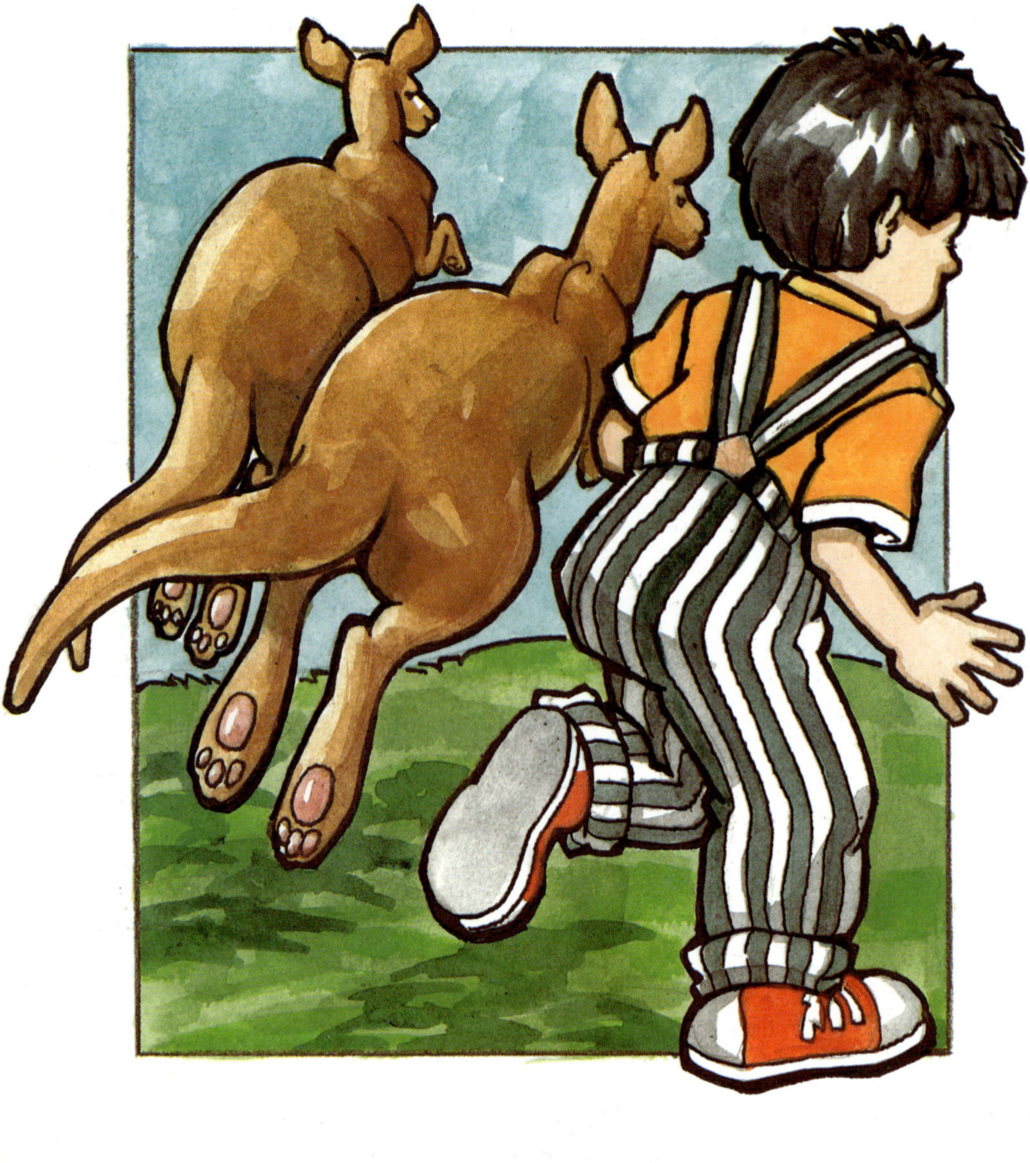

I can hop.

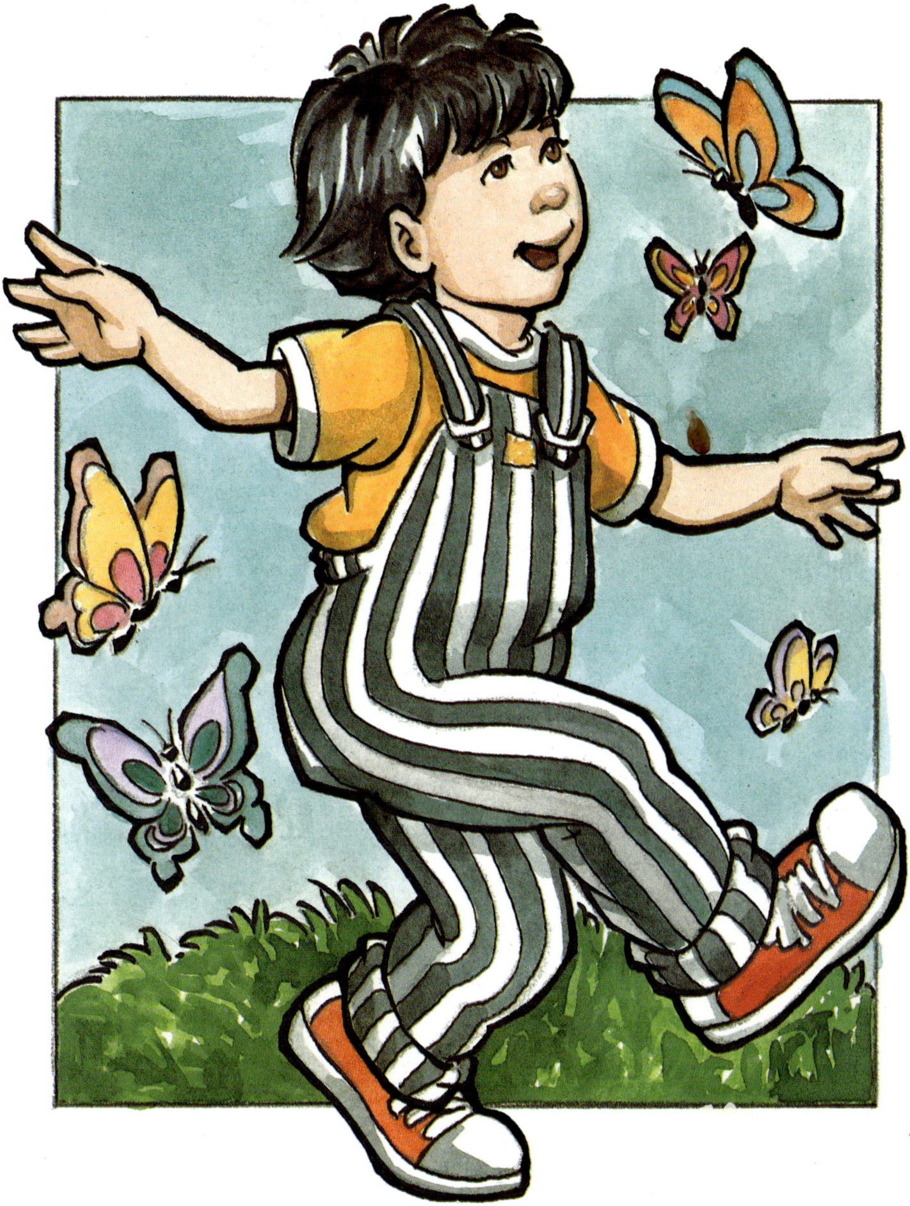

I can skip.

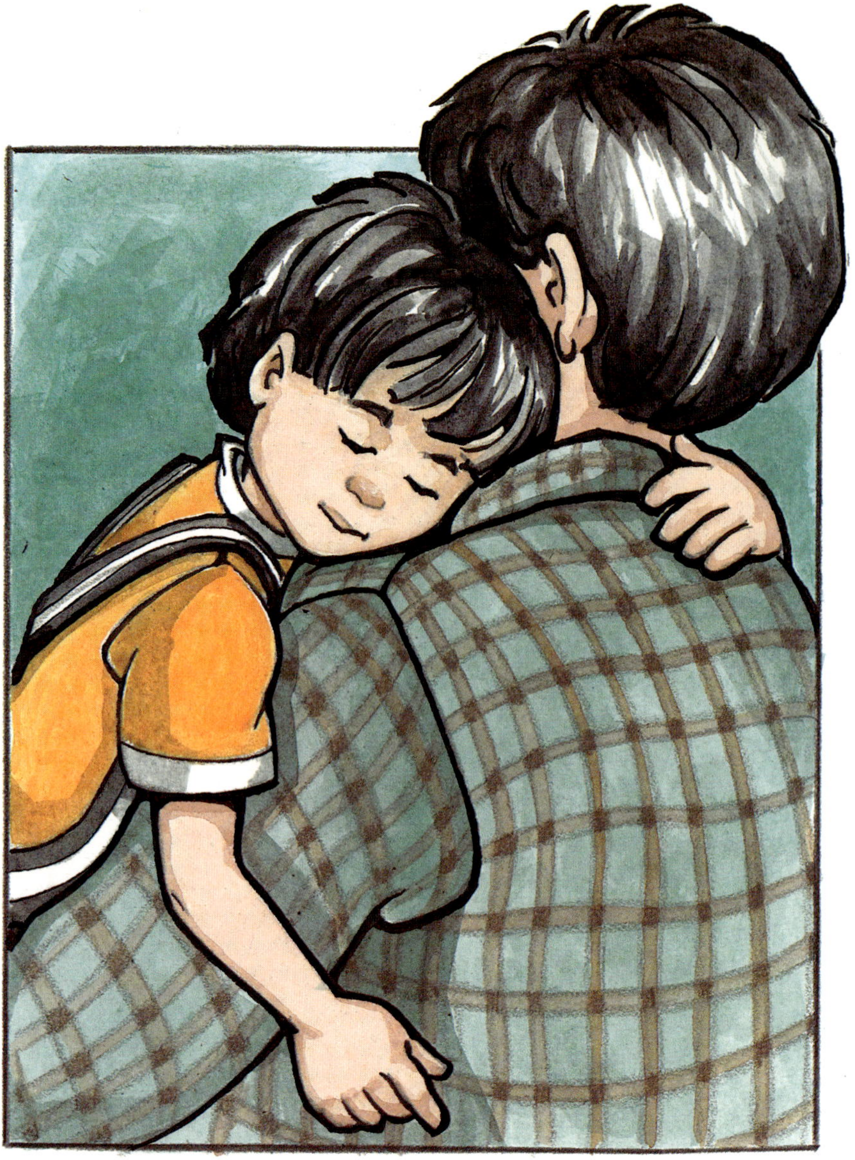

I can sleep.